THIS BOOK BELONGS TO

CW00515999

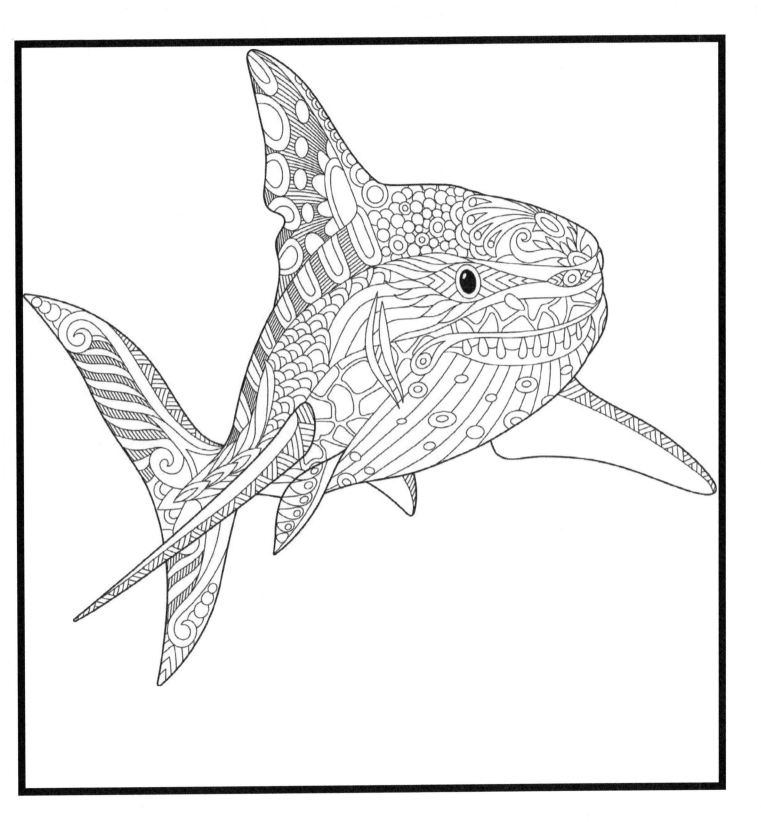

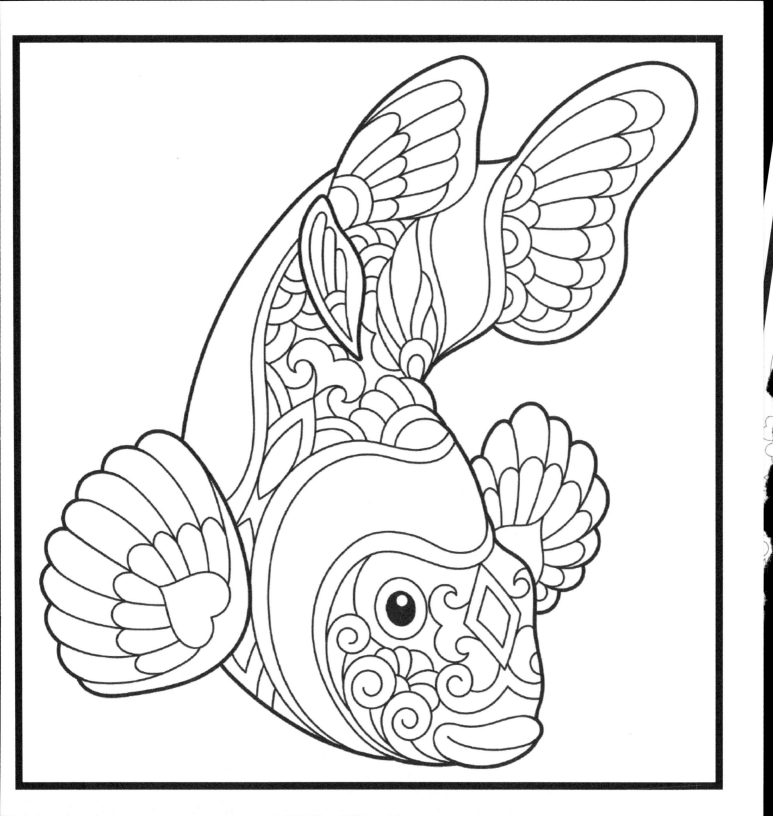

Hello, I'm Pippa and I want to express my gratitude for buying my book. As a small independent publisher your support means the world to me.

It would really be helpful if you could leave a review on Amazon, as all reviews for small businesses like mine can make a big difference. I'm curious as to why you bought this book and whether you liked it.

Thank you so much for your feedback.
Pippa

©Pippa Prais Designs

Printed in Great Britain
by Amazon

22178422R00059